The Art of
Mme. Jehane Benoit:
jams, pickles
& preserves

The Art of Mme. Jehane Benoit:
jams, pickles & preserves

*A selection of the finest recipes from
Canada's best known cook and authority
on Canadian foods.*

By

Jehane Benoit

Greywood Publishing Limited
101 Duncan Mill Road • Don Mills, Canada

CONTENTS

INTRODUCTION

In a book on fine preserves and clear jelly, published in 1901, I read: "Feeding your family on wholesome homemade jam, jelly and preserves brings health and happiness into each one of your everyday meals."

Specifically a preserved fruit is one that has been cooked in syrup until tender and transparent. The process is designed to obtain, as a final result, whole or cut-up pieces of fruit whose cells are filled with syrup replacing the natural juice of the fruit. Generally speaking, a preserve can be any fruit cooked in some manner with sugar — a jam, a conserve, a marmalade, or simply a fruit in syrup, — there is quite obviously more than one way to preserve fruits.

To complete the picture, remember that you can add your own touches that will give a special flavor to your preserving. I sometimes like to substitute part of the water I use with fresh orange or lemon juice, bottled cranberry juice, or juice extracted from fresh red or black currants. With pears I always add a slice of fresh ginger. I like a few grains of cardamom or coriander with any fruits. Peaches and strawberries must have a few fresh leaves of Rose Geranium. Apricots and cantaloups are quite special flavored with a few leaves of Sweet Cicely, and so on. I enjoy these but you may prefer something quite different, experiment and find out.

RULES FOR PRESERVING FRUIT
IN SYRUP

— Drop the prepared fruit into boiling syrup and cook over high heat until the fruit is transparent and tender. Remember that slow cooking dulls the fruit and makes in dark. Fruit preserved this way in syrup and packed while boiling hot into hot sterilized jars requires no further processing contrary to cold packed fruit, which must be processed.

— The general rule for sugar is to use from ¾ to 1 pound of sugar for each pound of fruit used. The sugar is added to the fruit in different ways, depending on the type of fruit used.
— Juicy berries may be sprinkled with the sugar and allowed to stand overnight. The sugar draws out the juices making enough liquid to form a syrup without the addition of any water.
— Juicy fruit with a firm skin, such as plums, cherries, etc., may be placed directly into a boiling hot medium syrup. As the natural juices of the fruit cook out, they thin the syrup to the right degree to let the syrup enter the cells of the fruit, which preserves it.
— Sour or acid fruit should be started in heavy syrup as there is no danger of crystallization since the acid

changes some of the sugar into a form which does not crystallize easily.

— It is when the fruit is tender and transparent that sugar syrup has replaced the fruit juice in the cells.

— Do your preserving by weight rather than by cups whenever possible as it is the only way to be accurate with fruit.

These are only a few of the basic rules and it is very important they are first understood in order to obtain any kind of results.

PRESERVES

BAKED PRESERVES

A Polish friend taught me how to make these; they have excellent keeping quality and retain all of their flavor. Equally good made with pears or peaches.

2½ lbs. of Damson plums
2½ lbs. sugar
1 lemon, thinly sliced

Wash plums, cut in halves and remove stones. Make alternate layers of plums, sugar and lemon slices in a baking dish. Cover and bake in a 350°F. oven for 3 hours (same time for pears or peaches). Remove from oven and pack in sterilized jars. Cool and cover with paraffin. Yield: 2½ pints.

PEACH AND ORANGE PRESERVE

Quick to prepare and cook, excellent keeping quality. In the winter, use it as a sandwich filling with cream cheese or to sweeten whipped cream and use as a cake topping.

6 large peaches
4 large oranges

1½ cups sugar
12 coriander seeds

Pour boiling water over the peaches, let stand 2 minutes, peel, remove pit and dice.

Peel the oranges and pass through food grinder.

Crush the coriander seeds with the back of a wooden spoon. Add to sugar. Mix together the peaches, ground oranges and sugar with coriander. Stir until well blended and let stand 1 hour. Bring to a full rolling boil over medium heat, stirring most of the time. Boil 30 minutes, stirring often, or until thick and golden color. Pour into hot sterilized jars, filling them to overflowing. Pour a coating of melted wax on top. Cool and seal. Yield: 2 pints.

PRESERVED PEARS

Preserved pears are never too exciting in flavor but this method of keeping our very good summer pears does quite a bit to make them glamourous. Equally good served plain as a dessert or on top of ice cream or sliced to fill a sponge cake or with roast turkey or baked ham.

1 lb. pears
1 cup pineapple juice
½ cup water
1½ cups sugar
1 unpeeled lemon, sliced paper thin
8 thin slices fresh ginger (optional)

Wash and peel the pears. Cut them in halves and remove the cores. Keep in cold water until ready to use.

Make a syrup with the pineapple juice, water and sugar. When the syrup comes to a full rolling boil, add the pears to the hot syrup one piece at a time so that the boiling will not stop. Cook until the pears are transparent and tender. The syrup should then register 224°F on a candy thermometer. Remove from heat and let the pears stand overnight in the syrup to plump them.

In the morning, bring back to a rapid boil, then pack the fruit only into hot, sterilized jars. Continue to boil the syrup until it comes again to 224°F on the thermometer. Fill the jars to overflowing with the hot syrup, add 2 slices of lemon and 2 slices of ginger to each jar and seal. Yield: 4 pints.

DAMSON PLUM PRESERVES

A marvellous recipe that gets everything possible out of this small, tart and tasty plum. The pits are easily removed once the jam is cooked.

4 to 5 cups Damson plums
2 cups sugar
¼ cup fresh orange juice
the grated peel of 1 orange
¼ cup water

Stem, wash and leave the plums whole. Place in a saucepan with the sugar, orange juice, grated rind and the water. Bring gently to a boil over medium heat, then simmer slowly until it has a jam consistency. Test by putting a teaspoon in a saucer, place in freezer or refrigerator. Only a few seconds are required to see if the jam sets in a sort of light jelly. Then remove from heat at once.

Remove the pits if you so wish. Pour into sterilized glasses. Seal. Keep in a dark, cool place. Yield: 3 8-ounce jam glasses.

OLD FASHIONED DAMSON PLUM PRESERVE

The blue Canadian Damson plums are one of our best fruits to preserve. They come and go quite fast so you must be aware of the moment when they are at their best and plentiful in the area you live in. Do not let the old trick of using vinegar in preserves deter you from trying this as they are the best Damson sweet I have ever made.

> 4 lbs. Damson plums
> 4 lbs. sugar
> ½ cup cider vinegar
> 1 pint water

Wash the plums, remove stems, but do not remove pit. Place whole plums into a saucepan, add the water and slowly bring to the boil, then boil until fruit bursts and is softened, about 10 minutes. Add the vinegar. Slowly bring back to the boil. While this is being done, divide the sugar on pie plates and warm it up in a 300°F oven. When the mixture boils, add the hot sugar and boil rapidly over high heat, stirring until all the sugar is dissolved and boil about 5 minutes or until set. Pour to overflowing into hot sterilized glasses. Wax is not necessary. Seal. Yield: 10 medium glasses.

THREE-FRUIT PRESERVE

This one is a must on my yearly list of preserving. Eating it in the middle of winter is just like bringing summer sunshine to your table. The syrup thickens quite a bit upon standing.

2 cups raspberries
2 cups strawberries
2 cups pitted cherries
sugar
½ cup lemon juice

Clean and mix together the raspberries, strawberries and cherries and weigh them. Sprinkle them with an equal weight of sugar, cover and let stand overnight. In the morning, place the fruits in a preserving kettle, add the lemon juice, bring to a boil, stirring most of the time, then cook over high heat until the fruit is clear and tender, this will take from 10 to 18 minutes. Cover and keep in a cool place overnight. In the morning, stir gently and pack into cold jars, sealing with melted paraffin. Yield: 6 to 8 half pints.

PRESERVED ORANGE SLICES

Serve with poultry, duck, goose, venison, etc., or use as topping on cottage cheese.

8 unpeeled oranges
4 cups sugar
1 cup cider vinegar
½ cup water
10 whole cloves
2 cinnamon sticks

Brush and slice oranges about ¼ inch thick, discard ends. Cover with water in a saucepan and simmer, covered, 1 hour or until tender. Drain, discarding the water.

Boil together 5 minutes the sugar, vinegar, water and spices. Add oranges and simmer 1 hour or until pieces are well glazed and almost transparent. Pack slices in hot sterilized jars. Cover with the hot syrup. Cool slightly and seal. Yield: 2 pints.

BEET PRESERVES

Surprisingly good with meat or as a dessert.

2 lbs. beets
4 cups sugar
1 tbsp. powdered ginger
1 cup slivered almonds
3 lemons, unpeeled, quartered and sliced

Cook the beets until tender in just enough water to cover. Drain, peel and dice finely.

Combine the beets with the sugar, ginger and almonds in a large saucepan. Simmer over very low heat about 30 minutes.

Add lemons, continue cooking 30 minutes longer. Pour into sterilized glasses. Yield: 6 8-oz. glasses.

ENGLISH MARROW PRESERVE

Making a good marrow preserve has been the pride of many an English homemaker as a perfect marrow preserve showed her skill in producing something really tasty from a food that there always seems to be too much of and a little on the dull side.

6 lbs. marrow (weigh when prepared)
6 lbs. sugar
rind and juice of 4 lemons
2 ounces dried ginger root

Cut the peeled marrow into 1 inch cubes. Place in a steamer or a large sieve, set over hot water, cover and steam about an hour or until the marrow is tender.

Pour the marrow into a bowl and add the grated lemon rind and juice. Break the ginger root by placing in a piece of cotton and hitting with a hammer. Place in a cheesecloth bag and add to the marrow. Stir in the sugar until thoroughly mixed and let stand for 24 hours. To cook, place the mixture in a large saucepan, simmer over medium heat until all the sugar is dissolved, then boil until the marrow is transparent and the syrup is thick. The time varies according to the amount of water in the marrow, it takes about 30 to 60 minutes to be right. Yield: 6 pints.

HONEY BUTTER

A Swiss specialty to serve with pancakes, French toast, gingerbread or muffins, to use as butter for cinnamon toast, or to top hot waffles. No matter where it is used, it is most tasty. Will keep 2 to 3 weeks, refrigerated, well covered.

½ cup butter
¼ cup honey, clear or granulated
½ cup heavy cream

Cream butter until very soft and creamy. Add honey and beat together for 5 minutes. Add cream a teaspoon at a time, beating constantly. Beat until smooth and fluffy. Store, well covered, in refrigerator.

For variation, flavor with the grated rind of half an orange or half a lemon.

BRANDIED CHERRIES

This world famous delight is easy to prepare and will keep 8 to 9 months in perfect condition. Keep in a cool, dark place.

2 lbs. sweet cherries, any type
2 cups sugar
2 cups water
brandy

Do not pit the cherries. The stems can even be left on the cherries, only then are they a little more difficult to pack.

Place them in a large bowl and cover with ice cold water. Let them stand 30 to 40 minutes. Drain and at this stage only should you remove the stems if you do not wish to leave them on.

Dissolve the sugar in the water, stirring all the time, then bring to a rolling boil. Boil rapidly for 5 minutes. Add the cherries and bring once more to a full rolling boil. Remove from heat, wait until the boiling stops and repeat this operation twice more, stirring gently with a wooden spoon.

Fill sterilized jars ¾ full of fruit and syrup, place cover loosely on jar and let stand until cool, then fill each jar with brandy. Stir in with a silver spoon. Seal. Turn jars upside down overnight. Then store in a cool dark place, right side up, for at least 3 months before using. Yield: about 4 pints.

OLD ENGLISH BRANDIED MINCEMEAT

Put these up in October in preparation for the Christmas holiday. You will have the finest pies.

2 lbs. lean round of beef
½ lb. ground beef suet
6 tart apples, unpeeled, chopped
5 cups sugar
2 tsp. coarse salt
1 tbsp. cinnamon
1 tbsp. nutmeg
1½ tsp. mace
1 tsp. allspice
1 lb. muscat raisins
1 lb. currants
¼ lb. candied orange peel
¼ lb. candied lemon peel
1 pint cider or orange juice
3 cups old port wine
1 cup brandy

Remove all fat from the meat, simmer until tender in salt water to cover. Cool and pass through meat chopper. Place in a large saucepan, add all the other ingredients except the brandy. Simmer 30 minutes, stirring often. Cool. Add the brandy. Pour into clean jars, cover and store in a cool place. Will keep 4 months. Yield: 5 quarts.

COUNTRY MINCEMEAT

Make in October for December.

1 lb. currants
½ lb. sultana raisins
1 lb. seedless raisins
2 lbs. apples
1 lb. beef suet, finely chopped
1½ lbs. dark brown sugar
½ lb. prunes, stoned and finely chopped
¼ lb. mixed peel
1 package (4 ounces) citron peel
grated rind of 2 lemons
juice of 3 lemons
1 tsp. almond essence
1 tsp. salt
1 tsp. cinnamon
1 tsp. nutmeg
½ tsp. powdered cloves
½ tsp. powdered ginger
1 cup red wine, brandy or apple juice

Clean and prepare all the ingredients. Put lemon juice, lemon rind and spices in a large bowl. Add prepared fruits, sugar and suet. Mix very thoroughly — the secret of perfect mincemeat is in the blending.

Add liquid of your choice gradually, while blending other ingredients without stopping. Of the different liquids suggested, brandy is definitely the best. Yield: 4 pints.

Place mincemeat in clean sterilized jars. Pour a thick layer of wax on each and seal at once. When stored in a cool dry cupboard, this mincemeat will keep for several months.

RASPBERRY VINEGAR

Easy to make, keeps 12 to 16 months in perfect condition, and makes a delicious beverage. Still made and enjoyed by the Mennonites and the French Canadians.

4 to 8 quart baskets of raspberries
white or cider vinegar
1 cup sugar to each cup of juice

Wash and crush the berries in a glass or earthenware bowl. Pour enough vinegar on top to cover the berries. Put a cloth on top and let stand 2 days in a cool place (do not refrigerate), it will not spoil.

Strain the juice through a double thickness of cheesecloth. Measure and add 1 cup sugar for each cup of juice. Place in a saucepan and boil 15 minutes, stirring until the sugar is dissolved. Pour into sterilized bottles. Seal and keep in a cool place.

To serve, put 2 to 4 tablespoons on top of ice cubes, fill glass with soda or plain water. Stir and serve. Yield: 3 pints.

RASPBERRY WINE VINEGAR

Another beverage made with raspberries, also very nice.

4 cups cleaned raspberries
1 cup cider or wine vinegar
1 cup Canadian red wine
1½ cups sugar

Cover the raspberries with the vinegar and wine and let stand 9 days. Keep well covered in a cool place.

Then pour the liquid and berries into a sieve and let drip for several hours. Add the sugar to the juice, simmer for 10 minutes, cool and bottle. Serve the same way as raspberry vinegar. Yield: 2 pints.

HOW TO MAKE GOOD JAMS
AND JELLIES

Jam making is not the laborious job that our mothers had. We have new methods, new ideas, countless helps, such as good bottled or canned juices, ready made pectine, frozen fruits, freezers and excellent refrigerators.

The first requirement of good jams and jellies is that they carry the flavor and bright color of the fruits they are made with.

Perfect jams are jelly-like in consistency, not stiff and sugary.

Jams must be fairly smooth because the fruit is crushed before cooking; that is why the soft textures of small fruit and berries are ideal for making jams. Jam is quicker and easier to make than jelly.

Perfect jelly is sparkling and clear. It has a slight quiver when unmolded, but will hold its shape. When jelly is cut with a spoon, it should retain the angle of the cut if the texture is perfect. Jelly should also be tender and easy to spread instead of leathery and almost unspreadable.

Too much sugar used in jams or jellies makes them sticky and sugary.

Unsound fruit, which is quite different from well ripened fruit, causes jam to ferment.

Scum left on jam or jelly also causes fermentation.

Jam and jelly, poured into hot, well sterilized jars and immediately covered, keep very well.

Four ingredients, in the right proportion, are most important in the making of any jam or jelly:—
1. Fruit   2. Acid   3. Pectin   4. Sugar.

Any fruit used in jams must have a balanced proportion of pectin and acid to transform the stewed fruit into jam. So, it is very important to know whether the pectin and acid are present naturally in the fruits or whether they must be added.

Underripe fruit contains more pectin than fully ripe fruit. Sharp apples, gooseberries, green currants and underripe plums have the most pectin, contrary to the best loved fruit for jam; strawberries have none, and that explains why there is so much failure in the making of strawberry jam, unless a perfectly well balanced recipe is followed.

However, it is well not to worry unduly about this as pectin is present in practically all fruit in fair quantity just before ripeness is reached, contrary to overripe fruit which has little but the combination of both green and ripe often helps. There is very good commercial powdered or liquid fruit pectin to facilitate this which is why some recipes use commercial pectin while others do not.

But even when pectin is present in fruit, it can only be made soluble by the acid in the fruit. Like pectin, acid varies in quantity, and underripe fruit contains more than ripe fruit. Here again, there is no problem since fresh lemon juice or citric acid (from the drugstore) will do the trick. One eighth of a teaspoon of citric acid is equal to one tablespoon lemon juice. To unify the pectin and acid present in fruit there is the sugar, which helps to jell the fruity mixture and is also a preservative and, of course, the heat or boiling.

If you are not sure of the pectin and acid content of the fruit, boil the fruit or juice a little longer before adding the sugar; this concentrates the juice and most of the time it will correct the deficiency.

It is easier to make small quantities of jam or jelly at a time, and it usually assures you of complete success. That is why the following recipes are for small quantities.

The fruit should be sound, ripe and some of it slightly underripe but never overripe.

Wash the fruit by putting it in a colander and letting the cold water from the tap run over it only as long as necessary as the less water on the fruit, the better. When making jam, boil the fruit gently until cooked before adding the sugar. Then, after the sugar is added, boil quickly for the shortest time possible, but until it jells. Overboiling fruit after adding sugar affects the flavor, color and consistency of the jam.

A very important fact to remember about sugar in jam making is that if it is added before the fruit boil, much more is needed as the acid turns the sugar to glucose.

35

After adding the sugar, stir well until it is dissolved. An old trick to prevent jam from sticking while cooking is to butter the bottom of the pan before starting.

Always pour jam into hot jars and apply wax coating while it is boiling hot.

With small berries, let the jam cool in the saucepan before pouring into the jar, it prevents the berries from rising.

Use a wooden spoon to stir. Use a metal spoon to remove scum as it accumulates around the edges.

An easy way to test doneness of jam or jelly is to place a few small plates in freezer. To test: put a small spoonful on the cold plate; let cool a few seconds; hold the plate vertically; if the jam remains on the plate, it is cooked.

When making jelly, cut the fruit large so the juice will flow more easily. Do not remove stalks, pips or seeds (they give pectin).

As a general rule, the prepared fruits are placed in a saucepan and just covered with water, then stewed until tender. Many a jelly has been spoiled by using too much water with the fruit.

When the fruit is tender, pour into a scalded jelly bag, placed over a bowl and suspended over the bowl after being tied. Let it drip 4 to 5 hours or overnight.

Then the juice is brought slowly to a fast rolling boil.

Warm up the sugar before adding to the fruit, place it on pie plates set in a 275°F. oven for 20 minutes.

The same as for jam, boil very fast once the sugar is added. Pot, wax and finish as for jam.

General Proportions for Jam

With these basic proportions, you can make your own jam with any fruits you like, in small or large quantities.

Fruit: 1 pound, weighed when prepared.

Sugar: ¾ pound or 1½ cups.

Apples and Other Fruit

Use ¾ pound apples and ¼ pound of other fruit, such as peaches, apricots, raspberries, etc.

This is just an example. Makes any desired combination of fruits.

When in doubt about pectin and acid content, use part apples, which are strong in both.

How to Proceed

Wash fruits, peel or dice or leave whole as necessary, weigh or measure. Place in saucepan adding just enough water barely to cover the bottom of the saucepan.

Heat slowly over low heat to avoid burning for about 15 minutes, crushing fruits if necessary.

Then add the sugar and simmer over low heat for 30 to 40 minutes or until thick. Time varies with the different types of fruit. Pour into hot jars, wax and seal.

JAMS AND CONSERVES

CARROT RHUBARB JAM

This tasty jam can be made all year round — with summer or winter rhubarb, with young or old carrots. Another fine point, it is just as nice freshly made as ripened.

3 cups carrots, grated
6 cups rhubarb, diced
grated rind and juice of 3 oranges
1 cup honey
½ tsp. salt
¼ tsp. nutmeg

Peel the carrots and grate on the fine grater. Place the diced rhubarb in a bowl, pour boiling water on to completely cover it. Let stand 10 minutes and drain. Add the carrots to the rhubarb, the orange rind and juice, the honey, salt and nutmeg.

Mix well. Cover and let stand overnight in a cool place. Do not use a metal bowl, unless it is stainless steel.

Next morning, bring the mixture to a boil. Cook over medium heat, stirring often, until the mixture is slightly thickened and the rhubarb is transparent. Remember it will be much thicker after it is completely cooled. Pour hot into sterilized jars and seal. Yield: 2½ pints.

MY MOTHER'S PLUM JAM

Although mother always called this a jam, it is truly a conserve. As children, we used to ask for the plum marmalade. Whichever name you give it. I think you will enjoy the sweet and sour quality of this jam.

3 lbs. blue plums
2 oranges, unpeeled
1 lemon, unpeeled
1 cup seedless raisins
sugar

Wash and cut up the plums. Remove the stones.

Cut the oranges and the lemon and put through the food grinder, removing the seeds before grinding to taste.

Add the raisins to the ground fruit and plums and measure the whole.

Measure 1 cup sugar for each cup of mixed fruits. Add to fruits. Simmer over low heat, stirring often, as the mixture is a bit dry at the beginning but soon a great deal of juice is formed. Remore scum as it accumulates. Cook until it becomes a thick consistency, remembering that it thickens quite a bit as it ages.

Pour while hot into jelly glasses or jars. Cover with wax. Yield: 6 jelly glasses.

PLUM AND APPLE JAM

An economical jam because during our plum season apples are always plentiful and cheap.

3 lbs. plums of your choice
3 lbs. apples
5½ lbs. sugar
2 cups water

Wash and cut a slit down one side of each plum with a knife.

Peel, core and slice the apples fairly thinly. Put in a saucepan with the water and simmer over low heat until the apples are almost tender. Beware of overcooking at this stage as during later stages the apples may become overcooked. When the apples are just tender at the edges, add the plums and simmer until the plums begin to soften and form juice.

Then add sugar cup by cup, stirring gently all the time. Continue stirring until the sugar is dissolved. Then boil fairly fast, removing the pits with a perforated spoon as they rise to the surface, and continue boiling until it meets the jam test on the cold plate. Yield: 8 to 9 jam jars.

OLD ENGLISH PLUM CONSERVE

The Old English has been modernized by using commercial pectin. The sour cling stone plums make the best conserve. If you use sweet blue plums or Italian damson plums, substitute ¼ cup fresh lemon juice for ¼ cup of the prepared plums. Omit the water and use 5 cups of sugar. This old recipe is worth trying.

4 cups prepared plums (about 2 quarts ripe plums)
1 cup seeded raisins
1 cup chopped nut meats
6 cups (2 lbs. 10 ounces) sugar
1 cup water
½ bottle fruit pectin

Pit (do not peel) about 2 quarts of fully ripe plums. Cut in pieces and chop. Measure 4 cups into a very large saucepan.

Add raisins, nut meats, sugar and water to fruit in a saucepan and mix well. Place over high heat, bring to a full rolling boil and boil hard 1 minute, stirring constantly. Remove from heat and at once stir in pectin. Skim off foam with a metal spoon. Then stir and skim by turns for 5 minutes to cool slightly and prevent the fruit from floating. Ladle quickly into glasses. Cover at once with ⅛ inch hot paraffin. Yield: about 12 medium glasses (6 lbs. of conserve).

PEACH APPLE JAM

The first duchess apples combined with ripe peaches make a perfect jam.

5 cups prepared fruit
(about 1½ lbs. ripe apples and 2½ lbs. ripe peaches)
1 tsp. grated lemon rind
2 - 3 lemons
6½ cups sugar
1 box fruit pectin crystals

First, prepare the fruit. Peel and core about 1½ lbs. of fully ripe tart apples. Chop fine. Peel and pit about 2½ lbs. of fully ripe peaches. Chop fine. Combine fruits and measure 5 cups into a very large saucepan. Grate the rind from 1 medium-sized lemon, measure 1 teaspoon, and add to fruit. Squeeze the juice from 2 or 3 lemons. Measure ⅓ cup into saucepan with fruit.

Then make the jam. Measure sugar and set aside. Add fruit pectin crystals to fruit in saucepan and mix well. Place over high heat and stir until mixture comes to a hard boil. At once stir in sugar. Bring to a full rolling boil and boil hard 1 minute, stirring constantly. Remove from heat. Skim off foam with a metal spoon. Then stir and skim by turns for 5 minutes to cool slightly and prevent the fruit from floating. Ladle quickly into glasses. Cover at once with ⅛ inch hot paraffin. Yield: 11 medium glasses.

24-HOUR STRAWBERRY JAM

The time involved is more than worth it.

**4 cups large strawberries
5 cups sugar
3 tbsp. lemon juice**

Place 1 cup cleaned strawberries in a saucepan. Sprinkle 1 cup sugar on top. Repeat until all strawberries and sugar have been used. Slowly bring to the boil and simmer 9 minutes, stirring as little as possible.

Remove from heat, add the lemon juice. Let rest overnight (do not leave in metal pan, except enamelled cast iron).

The following day, bring back to the boil over high heat. Simmer again for 9 minutes over low heat. Remove from heat. Remove scum. Cool slightly. Pour into hot sterilized jars. Seal at once. Yield: 6 6-oz. jars.

TOMATO-LEMON JAM

An old fashioned preserve, that never loses its appeal. My grandmother, who showed me how to do it, used red or yellow tomatoes.

5 lbs. firm tomatoes
5 lbs. sugar
3 unpeeled lemons, sliced thin
1 tbsp. grated fresh ginger root or 1 tsp. ground ginger

Peel and cut up tomatoes coarsely. Place in a saucepan in alternate layers with the sugar and lemon slices. Add the ginger (when possible use the fresh ginger root). Simmer slowly over medium low heat, stirring frequently until thick, about 45 to 50 minutes. It must have the consistency of jam. Pour into hot sterilized glasses. Seal at once. Makes about 4 to 5 (6-oz.) glasses.

MAMAN'S RASPBERRY JAM

This perfect raspberry jam has been failure-proof for 40 years. As soon as the ripe red raspberries appear on the market, I make a few glasses as my mother did before me.

4 cups raspberries
1 tbsp. vinegar
4 cups sugar

Place the berries in a sieve and quickly run under cold water. This is important as they easily absorb water, and too much would spoil the jam. Remove the stems and measure. Place in a large saucepan with the vinegar. Bring to boil, without stirring, over medium heat, then boil 5 minutes.

Measure and place the sugar in 3 pie plates. Heat in a 275°F. oven for 20 minutes. Add the hot sugar to the berries, which have boiled for 5 minutes, one plate at a time. Adding the hot sugar this way does not stop the boiling. Then boil exactly 2 minutes over high heat. Pour into hot sterilized jars. Wax and seal. Yield: 4 to 5 jelly glasses.

APRICOT RASPBERRY JAM

Years ago, in Maryland, I tasted this jam and I have made it ever since. It is an old specialty of the South, usually served with hot flaky buttered biscuits and tea flavored with a rose petal placed on top of each cup.

> 2 lbs. fresh ripe apricots
> 2 cups fresh raspberries
> 2¼ lbs. sugar
> ¼ cup water
> 1 tbsp. lemon juice

Wash, peel and pit the apricots. Wash and clean the raspberries. Mix the fruits and add the sugar and water. Cool slowly, stirring occasionally, until thick. Test by putting a little on a cold refrigerated plate. When the syrup stiffens as soon as it is cool, the jam is done. Add the lemon juice. Stir a few seconds. Pour into hot sterilized jars. Seal with paraffin. Yield: 4 jelly glasses.

APRICOT CONSERVE

Apricots and pineapple are perfect companions.

1 quart chopped apricots
1 cup crushed pineapple
grated rind and juice of 2 oranges
grated rind and juice of 1 lemon
dash of salt
sugar to measure

Combine apricots, pineapple with juice, rinds and juice of oranges and lemon, and salt in heavy kettle. Cook 20 minutes, stirring occasionally. Measure pulp and add ¾ cup sugar for each cup of fruit.

Stir until sugar is dissolved, then cook rapidly until consistency is right for jam, about 20 minutes. Ladle into sterilized jars and seal. Yield: about 3 pints.

CHERRY RASPBERRY CONSERVE

Whole cherries, any type, add flavor and texture to this old fashioned favorite. Serve it sometimes with boiled ham or roasted turkey.

6 cups pitted cherries
2 cups red or black raspberries
2⅔ cups sugar

Pit and measure cherries, place in a saucepan with the raspberries and sugar. Stir until well mixed, then cook over medium heat, until thick, about 20 to 30 minutes. Stir often, as there is no liquid and this jam must make its own syrup. Pour into sterilized jars. Seal. Yield: 2 pints.

CRANBERRY FRUIT CONSERVE

Perfect to make in late autumn when fresh cranberries are on hand.

4 cups fresh cranberries
1½ cups water
2½ cups sugar
1 cup seeded raisins, chopped
1 apple, peeled, cored and chopped
grated rind and juice of 1 orange and 1 lemon
1 cup chopped walnuts (optional)

Cook cranberries in water until all the skins pop open, about 10 - 15 minutes. Add the remaining ingredients, except the walnuts. Bring back to boil, boil 15 minutes. Remove from heat, add the walnuts. Pack into hot sterile jars and seal with melted paraffin. Yield: 4 8-oz. glasses.

THREE-FRUIT JAM

Fresh rhubarb, pineapple and stawberries make an old fashioned June jam that never ceases to be delicious. Make only a batch at a time — the result is better.

3 cups shredded fresh pineapple
2 cups peeled and diced summer rhubarb
4 cups hulled strawberries
pinch of salt
juice of 1 lemon
4½ cups sugar

Grate the pineapple on medium grater. Place in a large preserving kettle and cook over medium heat for 10 minutes. Add the rhubarb, berries, salt and lemon juice, bring to a boil, then boil gently for 20 minutes.

Divide the sugar on pie plates, place in a 325°F. oven until sugar is quite hot. Add to fruit, boil rapidly, stirring often, for 20 to 25 minutes. Skim off foam and pour into hot sterilized jars. Seal with hot paraffin. Cover and store in a cool place. Yield: 6 half-pint jars.

JELLIES

CRABAPPLE JELLY

Superb for jelly, flavor to taste by adding to each jar a whole clove or a small piece of cinnamon stick or a rose petal.

Cut washed and stemmed crabapples into rough pieces. Add cold water barely to cover, simmer covered until fruit is soft, about 15 to 20 minutes. Drain through moistened jelly bag.

Measure juice and set aside ¾ cup sugar for each cup of juice. Boil juice uncovered about 3 to 5 minutes. Gradually add sugar, stirring until sugar is dissolved. Boil rapidly until two thick drops of syrup will run together and sheet off metal spoon.

Remove from heat, let stand 1 minute, skim. Pour into sterilized glasses. When cool, cover with a layer of melted paraffin, top with a clean lid.

WINTER APPLE JELLY

Easy to make and lovely to have on hand.

2 lbs. winter apples
juice of 2 lemons
grated rind of 1 lemon
1 lb. warm sugar per pint of juice

Wash the apples, cut in four, do not peel or core. Place in a saucepan with the lemon juice and rind. Add just enough cold water to barely cover the apples. Bring to the boil and simmer until the apples are tender.

Pour into a jelly bag and let drip 12 hours.

Measure the juice, bring to a full rolling boil, add the measured warmed sugar. Stir until the sugar is dissolved then boil at a full rolling boil 5 to 8 minutes or until it passes the jelly test. Pour into hot sterilized jelly glasses, cool slightly and seal. Yield: 6 8-oz glasses.

PLUM MINT JELLY

Perfect served with roasted lamb or chicken. Serve as a treat with creamed or cottage cheese. Nice on fruit salad. Almost a must in your jam cupboard.

3 lbs. ripe plums, any type
8 cups water
2 lbs. sour apples
sugar
1 cup fresh mint leaves

Place plums in a saucepan with 4 cups of the water, boil until the plums are soft. Cut the apples without peeling or coring, place in saucepan with the remaining 4 cups of water, boil until soft, then add to the plums, and stir together until well mixed. Pour into a jelly bag, hang over a bowl and let the juice drip through. Then measure juice, bring to a fast rolling boil, add sugar, cup for cup. When the sugar is dissolved, add the mint tied in a cheesecloth bag and hang from the handle of pan. Boil until it reaches the jelly test. Then remove mint, pressing juice out on side of pan. Skim jelly, pour into sterilized glasses. Seal. Yield: 6 to 8 jelly glasses.

DAMSON PLUM JELLY AND BUTTER

Damsons are the first choice for this 2 in 1 recipe, but any bright colored, tart plums can be used.

4 cups plum juice
3 cups sugar

To obtain juice, cover 6 to 8 pounds plums with cold water, hold the plums down with one hand and pour out the water until it just covers them. Then boil, uncovered, over medium heat until the plums are very soft. Turn them into a jelly bag and let the juice drip overnight.

In the morning, measure the 4 cups of juice, add the sugar, bring to the boil, stirring until the sugar is dissolved. Then boil steadily until the syrup sheets from the spoon or to a jelly consistency. Skim, pour into sterilized jars, seal with paraffin. Cover. Yield: 4 to 6 jelly glasses.

To Make the Plum Butter:

Put the plum pulp (removing all the pits possible) left in the bag through a food mill, measure and add ⅔ cup sugar for each cup of pulp, and cook over low heat until thick, stirring often, so it will not scorch. To taste, flavor with ¼ teaspoon cinnamon for each ⅔ cup sugar. Pour into jars and seal.

HONEY JELLY

A clear amber color delicious jelly, that can be made any time during the year. I love it with bran muffins or my morning toast, when wholewheat bread is used.

2½ cups clear honey
¾ cup strained fresh lemon juice
½ cup bottled pectin

Blend the honey and lemon juice in a large saucepan (it foams quite a bit, when it cooks). Bring to a full rolling boil over medium heat, stirring constantly. Add the pectin, while stirring bring again to full boil and boil 1 minute. Remove from heat. Skim and pour into sterilized jelly glasses. Cover with paraffin while hot. Yield: 5 jelly glasses.

PORT WINE AND GRAPE JELLY

A must with jugged hare and roasted duck.

3 cups sugar
1 box powdered pectin
½ cup bottled grape juice
1½ cups port wine
1 cup water

Measure the sugar in a bowl. Mix the pectin with the juice, port and water, in a saucepan. Stir until pectin is dissolved, then place over high heat and stir until the mixture comes to a full rolling boil.

Add the sugar at once and return to a hard boil. Boil 1 minute, stirring constantly. Remove from heat, skim off the foam and pour at once into hot sterile jars. Seal. Yield: 6 to 7 6-oz. glasses.

GRAPEFRUIT WINE JELLY

Unusual and delicious. Superb with roast turkey or baked ham. Very good with hot toasted muffins or crumpets. A gourmand's treat, done in 10 minutes.

1 cup fresh grapefruit juice
1 cup port wine
3½ cups sugar
½ bottle (3 ounces) liquid pectin

In a saucepan combine the freshly squeezed strained grapefruit juice, the wine and sugar. Stir over low heat until the sugar is all dissolved, this will take about 8 to 10 minutes. Remove from heat and stir in the pectin. Skimming is necessary. Pour immediately into hot sterilized jars and seal with paraffin. Yield: 5 jelly glasses.

FRESH PARSLEY JELLY

Other herb jellies can be made in the same manner, replacing the parsley with an equal quantity of any herb you choose.

2 cups parsley, tightly packed
2¼ cups cold water
2 tbsp. lemon juice
green vegetable coloring
3½ cups sugar
½ bottle (6 oz.) commercial pectin

Wash the parsley and place in a saucepan. Crush with a masher for a few seconds to extract some of the oil. Add the water and slowly bring to the boil. Remove from the heat, cover and let rest 10 minutes. Pass through a jelly bag. The yield should be 1½ cups.

Place the parsley infusion in a saucepan, add the sugar and enough green vegetable coloring to give a nice color. Mix well.

Bring to the boil, while stirring, until the sugar is melted. Then bring to a fast rolling boil. Add the pectin. Boil exactly 1 minute while stirring. Remove the scum. Place a sprig of parsley into each hot jelly glass. Fill with the hot jelly, cool slightly and seal. Yield: 6 jelly glasses.

UNCOOKED JAMS AND JELLIES

THIS IS THE MODERN WAY OF MAKING
JAMS AND JELLIES

Not only are these uncooked jams less work than the long cooking methods, I find they have better color, and a most pleasant taste and smell of fresh fruit, probably because they are made with fully ripe fruit and are not cooked.

Because they are not cooked, they must be made with commercial pectin, and they must have time to set. They can be made into jams or jellies, with fresh fruits, or frozen juice concentrates, or bottled juice. They must be refrigerated or kept in freezer. Once opened, still keep refrigerated and use.

APPLE JELLY

Easy to make apple jelly without apples!

**1 box powdered fruit pectin
2 cups (1½ pts.) canned apple juice
a few drops red food coloring
3½ cups (1½ lbs.) granulated sugar**

Scald five 6-oz. jelly glasses.

In a large saucepan, mix pectin with apple juice and enough red food coloring to tint the mixture a light orange.

Stir over high heat until mixture comes to a hard boil; stir in sugar at once. Bring to a full, rolling boil; boil hard 1 minute, stirring constantly. Remove from heat.

With metal spoon, skim off foam. Fill glasses. Cool and refrigerate. Yield: 4-5 jelly glasses.

CHERRY JELLY

Rarely can we buy a good cherry jelly, yet it is so nice to serve for tea with cream cheese and hot rolls or with ham or fruit salad. This is an uncooked jelly made with fresh fruits. A fruit of your choice can replace the cherries.

4¾ cups sugar
3 cups fresh cherry juice
1 package powdered fruit pectin
½ cup water

No matter what method is used, you must first extract the fruit juice, but that is easy. Wash the fruit. Place in a saucepan. Add just a little water to cover the bottom of the pan. Boil rapidly 10 to 15 minutes, crushing the fruit as you boil. Pour into a bag and let it drip as previously explained. Measure juice. Add the sugar to 1¼ cups of the cherry juice. Stir until sugar is well mixed.

Slowly add the water to the powdered pectin. Heat, *just* to the boiling point, stirring constantly. Pour this hot pectin into the remaining cherry juice, and stir until the pectin is thoroughly mixed. Let stand 15 minutes, stirring 2 to 3 times.

Add the sugar mixture, stir until the sugar is dissolved.

Pour into jelly glasses. Cover with tight lids. Let stand on kitchen counter until set, this may take from 6 to 14 hours. It will harden still more after it sets, when refrigerated.

Freeze or refrigerate. Yield: 5 to 6 jelly glasses.

MINT-CURRANT JELLY

Minute-style jelly.

2 tsp. fresh mint leaves, chopped
½ tsp. grated orange rind
1 glass (6 ounces) currant jelly

Place chopped fresh mint, grated orange rind and currant jelly in a small saucepan. Stir gently over hot water until well blended. Pour jelly back into glass. Cover.

Let stand 24 hours in refrigerator before serving. The same can be done with any fragrant herb of your choice and all jams, jellies or honey.

GRAPE JELLY

This jelly is made with bottled juice. Therefore, the first part of cooking to make the juice, as with cherry jelly, is eliminated. Serve it with chicken or roast pork.

1 package powdered fruit pectin
2 cups lukewarm water
1 (6-oz.) can frozen grape juice concentrate
3¼ cups sugar

Pour the lukewarm water into a large bowl, gradually add the powdered fruit pectin, stirring all the time. Stir until completely dissolved. Let stand 45 minutes, stirring gently occasionally.

Pour the thawed out, but cold, undiluted concentrated grape juice into a bowl. Add 1½ cups of the sugar. Mix thoroughly and stir until the sugar is partly dissolved.

Add remaining 1¾ cups sugar to the dissolved pectin. Stir until the sugar is dissolved. Add the juice mixture to the pectin. Stir until sugar is dissolved. Pour into containers. Cover with lids. Let stand on kitchen counter about 24 hours or until set. Refrigerate. Yield: 5 to 6 jelly glasses.

UNCOOKED PEACH JAM

The full peach flavor and color are preserved.
2½ pounds peaches
5 cups sugar
1 package powdered pectin
1 cup water

Remove skins and pits from fully ripe peaches, and crush peaches with a fork or potato masher. Stir in sugar well, and let the mixture stand 20 minutes, stirring occasionally.

Cook powdered pectin and water together to the boiling point, then boil for 1 minute. Accurate timing is very important here. Add pectin to peach mixture, and stir 2 minutes. Again, correct timing is important.

Then ladle the jam into nine 6-ounce sterilized jelly glasses, and let stand at room temperature 24 to 48 hours. Cover with a layer of paraffin, and store in refrigerator or freezer.

This delicious, fresh-tasting jam must be kept cold. You'll notice the consistency is not so thick as in commercial jams. Yield: 9 6-oz. glasses.

BLUEBERRY JAM

Do not use large cultivated berries to make this jam as the small natural blueberries have more flavor. Try them in the winter as a sponge cake filling, topped with whipped cream.

> ½ cup powdered fruit pectin
> 4 tbsp. sugar
> 2 cups blueberries
> 1½ cups sugar
> 4 tbsp. corn syrup
> 4 tbsp. lemon juice

Place the powdered fruit pectin and the 4 tablespoons of sugar in the bowl of an electric mixer. Stir together with a spoon until well mixed. Add the blueberries. Crush in the sugar, then beat, at low speed, for 7 minutes.

Add the 1½ cups sugar, the corn syrup and lemon juice. Beat at low speed for 3 more minutes. Pour into freezer container. Cover. Let stand on kitchen counter for 12 hours or until set into a soft jelly. Freeze. Yield: 4 half pint containers.

NO-COOKING STRAWBERRY JAM

This jam, of a deep rose color with a flavor of freshly picked strawberries, is not a food pleasure that can be made in large quantities as it must be refrigerated to keep (4 to 5 months in the fridge or 8 to 10 months in the freezer.)

5 cups sugar
3 cups crushed strawberries
1 package powdered or granulated pectin
1 cup water

Add sugar to crushed fruits. Mix well. Let stand 20 minutes stirring occasionally. Dissolve the pectin in cold water, bring to a boil. Boil 1 minute. Add pectin solution to the fruits and sugar and stir for 2 minutes.

Ladle jam into jelly glasses, cover, let stand on kitchen counter until set or jellied, which may take from 24 to 48 hours. Seal, cover and keep in refrigerator or freezer. Yield: 6 8-oz. jars.

QUICK FREEZE PLUM JAM

This jam does not have the deep red color of a cooked plum jam, it is amber with dark red pieces of skin. The flavor is superb the work really easy. It must be kept refrigerated and will keep for 6 to 8 weeks. For a longer period, it has to be frozen.

2 cups prepared freestone plums
4 cups sugar
1 package powdered fruit pectin
1 cup water
juice of 1 lemon

To prepare fruits, wash, pit and put through a food chopper. Measure. Place in a glass bowl, add sugar, stir to mix and let stand for 20 minutes, stirring occasionally.

Place in a saucepan the pectin and water. Bring to a boil, and boil rapidly for 1 minute, stirring constantly. Remove from heat. Add lemon juice and sugared fruits, stir for 2 minutes. Pour into clean jars and cover. Let stand at room temperature for 1 hour. Refrigerate until jam is set. Store in freezer. Once opened, keep refrigerated. Yield: 5 to 6 half pints.

RULES FOR MAKING MARMALADE

Homemade marmalade is not only better, it is also much cheaper than the mass produced variety. To be perfect, it should have a tangy or piquant taste. The best known marmalades contain citrus fruits, but many excellent types are made from other fruit and combinations of fruit. However, they are always flavored with one or the other of the citrus fruits. In a good marmalade the fruit appears to be suspended in a clear jelly syrup. Another advantage of marmalade is that, unlike some jams, it needs little time to mature and mellow in flavor.

The best fruit for making marmalade is just slightly underripe because at this stage the pectin and acid content is still high, an essential if we are to get the marmalade to set. Pectin is a natural gum-like substance present, to some extent, in most fruits before they are quite ripe. All citrus fruit has a high pectin content.

The following are the basic rules for making marmalade.

— In most marmalades the peels are made tender before the sugar is added. Often the pips are soaked overnight to extract their natural pectin.

- It is best to warm up the sugar, the same as for jams and jellies.
- Wait until the sugar is completely dissolved before boiling briskly, then stir gently and slowly quite often until the marmalade sets when tested. Boiling for too long darkens the color and spoils the flavor.
- To test the cooking point, remove pan from heat, and spoon a little onto a cold plate (as for jams and jellies). Another trick is to use the metal underside of an ice cube tray, straight from the refrigerator. Use either way so that no time is wasted waiting for the marmalade to cool. Run your finger through the center and if the marmalade is ready, the surface will crinkle and remain in two separate portions.
- Skimming the foam from around the pan should be done only towards the end of cooking, it is usually best to do it after testing. Continuous skimming is unnecessary and wasteful. To remove the scum use an ordinary tablespoon, dipped in boiling water before each operation.
- Have jars sterilized, dry and warm before filling. If you have a dishwasher, put in your jars while the marmalade cooks. Fill jars quite full to allow for shrinkage.
- Label jars with the name and date. The best labels are sensitive Skin Tape "Dermicel". They are quickly put on and easy to write on; use a ballpoint pen to mark them. Even when washed in an automatic dishwasher, they stay on.
- The two most common faults found in homemade marmalade are mould on the top and crystallization. Mould is usually caused by air being allowed to reach

the marmalade, owing to imperfect covering. Mould is usually a yeast growing there, feeding on the sugar. When the jars are airtight, the spores of yeast cannot gain access. Filling to overflowing prevents this.

Crystallization of the sugar is usually due to not having stirred sufficiently when it was first added to the fruit so that some of the sugar remains undissolved.

Buying Tips on Citrus Fruits

— Navel oranges are on the market from November to May.

— Valencia oranges from February to November.

— Bitter Seville oranges from January to early April.

— Jaffa oranges are an early spring fruit.

— Lemons are available throughout the year.

— Grapefruits have two seasons — from October to June and from June to September. The winter citrus fruits make a better marmalade.

— Tangerines are available from November to April.

— Japanese mandarins are available from December to early February.

3 to 4 medium oranges	= 1 cup juice
2 medium oranges	= 1 cup bite-sized pieces
1 medium orange	= 4 teaspoons grated peel
6 medium lemons	= 1 cup juice
1 medium lemon	= 3 teaspoons grated peel
1 medium grapefruit	= ⅔ cup juice
1 medium grapefruit	= 10 to 12 sections

MARMALADES

CARTWHEELS MARMALADE

To make unpeeled citrus cartwheels — wash fruits, trim a thin slice from both ends, then slice fruit crosswise very thinly, or more thickly, according to recipe. For half cartwheels, cut slice in half.

3 medium oranges, unpeeled
1 medium lemon, unpeeled
12 cups cold water
sugar

Thinly slice unpeeled oranges and lemons, cut into half cartwheels. You should have 3 cups of oranges and ¾ cup of lemon — if not, add what is necessary.

Place fruit in a large glass bowl, pour cold water on top. Cover and let stand overnight. In the morning, place in an earthenware bowl with the water, juice and bring to a rolling boil. Boil hard, uncovered, for 30 minutes or until the water is reduced to 8 cups. Let rest 6 to 8 hours.

Then measure fruit and liquid and measure an equal amount of sugar. Bring the juice to a rolling boil, warm up the sugar in a 250°F. oven. Add to the boiling juice. Boil, while stirring, until sugar dissolves. Then boil until the marmalade sets when tested, about 30 minutes. Remove from heat. Skim for 5 minutes. Pour into hot sterilized jars and seal with paraffin. Yield: 6 to 7 jelly glasses.

SEVILLE ORANGE MARMALADE

Smooth, tart, beautiful — perfect for those who like a not too sweet marmalade.

8 tangy or bitter Seville oranges
3 medium-sized sweet oranges
2 medium-sized lemons
18 cups water
8 lbs. sugar

Cut the unpeeled oranges and lemons in half, squeeze out the juice. Strain and put the pips in a small cheesecloth bag. Cut the yellow peel and the pulp (not the white part) of the oranges and lemons into fine shreds. Place in an earthenware bowl with the water, juice and bag of pips. Cover and let soak 24 hours. Then pour all of it into a large enamel cast iron pan. Tie the bag of pips to the handle of saucepan for easy removal and bring to a rolling boil, then boil uncovered until the mixture is reduced by half. This will take 1½ to 2 hours.

Warm up the sugar, remove the bag of pips and add the sugar, dissolved over medium heat, while stirring constantly, then boil rapidly about 30 minutes or until the marmalade sets when tested. Skim. Pour into warm dry jars. Seal with paraffin. Yield: 10 16-oz. jars.

LEMON MARMALADE

From the same recipe, I make a variation by adding 1 large fresh ginger root, grated, to the lemon cartwheels. The result is a tangy, delicious lemon ginger marmalade.

6 lemons, unpeeled
7 cups cold water
sugar

Slice the unpeeled lemons, as thinly as possible, then cut into half cartwheels. Then measure, you should have 4 cups. Place in a glass or earthenware bowl, cover with the cold water and let stand 24 hours.

When ready, pour into a large enamel cast iron saucepan, and bring to a full rolling boil. Boil rapidly, uncovered, for 25 minutes. Then measure the fruit and liquid, it should then be about 5½ cups; whatever you have, add an equal quantity of warm sugar. Return to heat, and stir until the sugar is dissolved. Then boil rapidly until marmalade sets when tested. Pour into hot sterilized jars and seal with paraffin. Yield: 5 to 6 jelly glasses.

THREE-FRUIT MARMALADE

A marmalade that can always be on hand for a gift from your kitchen, a thank-you note, or just for your pleasure because you can make it anytime of the year.

3 grapefruits
3 oranges
3 lemons
water
sugar

Choose thin skinned, medium-sized fruits and wash. First, quarter each unpeeled fruit, then slice very thinly, saving the pips and the juice.

Measure the fruit and place in large non-metal bowl, then add 3 times the quantity of cold water. Add the pips tied in a bag. Let stand 24 hours. Then squeeze the pips to release any liquid and pectin they contain, and discard.

Place in a large saucepan and boil, uncovered, for 2 hours. Then again measure quantity in pan as before and add an equal quantity of warmed up sugar. Stir over gentle heat until all the sugar has dissolved, then boil rapidly until the marmalade sets when tested.

Remove from heat, skim and let stand 1 hour. Stir well to distribute the peel evenly , then pour into warm jars and cover at once. Yield: 8 8-oz. jars.

GRAPEFRUIT MARMALADE

This is a thin shred type of marmalade. If you have a special little knife, called a stripper, to make long thin strips, it makes a beautiful marmalade. If not, cut with scissors or make long shreds on fine shredder.

> 1 big ripe grapefruit
> 1 medium lemon
> cold water
> sugar

Strip the peel of the fruits, using only the yellow part. Put the pulp and white of the rind through the food chopper, using the coarsest blade and removing the pits as you go.

Combine the ground pulp and the sliced rind and measure. Add 3 times as much cold water. Let stand 12 hours.

The next morning boil for 15 minutes and let stand again overnight. On the third morning measure what you have. Bring to a fast rolling boil. Measure and heat an equal quantity of sugar and add to mixture. Stir until sugar is dissolved, then boil until the marmalade sets when tested.

Let it cool, then stir it well once more. Pour into sterilized jars and seal with paraffin. Yield: about 10 jelly glasses.

LIME MARMALADE

To make this unusual and delicious marmalade, you will have to do a few things over a span of 3 or 4 days, so take this into account when you begin. The recipe can be done with 2 as well as 24 limes.

limes
cold water
sugar

The first day: Take as many fresh limes as you like and peel off the outer green skin, very thin. If you have a stripper knife, use it to make thin shreds of the green skin, instead of peeling. Without a stripper knife, slice the rind in long thin shreds with a sharp knife or scissors.

Slice the peeled limes and put through meat chopper, removing the seeds.

Measure the rind and the pulp and cover them with

3 times as much cold water. Wrap the pips and add. Let soak overnight.

The second day: Boil the mixture for 15 minutes and let stand, again overnight.

The third day: Measure again and place in saucepan. Measure an equal quantity of sugar. Bring to a fast rolling boil. Heat the sugar and add to the juice, stir until the sugar is dissolved. Then boil until the marmalade sets when tested. Let stand overnight.

The fourth day: Stir the marmalade to distribute the rind evenly. Pour into jars and seal with paraffin.

RHUBARB MARMALADE

A springtime must.

> juice of 2 oranges
> juice of 1 lemon
> finely grated rind of 2 oranges
> 6 cups diced rhubarb
> 6 cups sugar
> pinch of salt
> 1 cup seedless sultana raisins

Place in a saucepan in the following order the orange juice, lemon juice, grated orange rind, cleaned and diced rhubarb, sugar and salt. Slowly bring to the boil, stirring most of the time. Boil 10 minutes.

Add the raisins. Boil until the jam has the right consistency. Stir often and cook over medium heat. Pour into hot sterilized jars, cool slightly and seal. Yield 8 8-oz. jars.

RIPE TOMATO MARMALADE

The citrus fruits are there, but the tomatoes are the *prima donna*.

3 quarts (12 cups) peeled and sliced tomatoes
6 cups sugar
1 tsp. salt
2 oranges
2 lemons
2 cups water
4 sticks cinnamon
2 tsp. whole cloves

Mix the tomatoes, sugar and salt in a large saucepan and set aside.

Peel the oranges and lemons, removing the white part. Cut the peels into small slivers. Place in a saucepan, cover with cold water, bring to a boil, boil 5 minutes. Drain and add peels to tomatoes. Cut the orange and lemon pulp into small pieces, remove the seeds and add the fruit to the tomatoes.

Tie the cinnamon and cloves in cheesecloth and also add to tomatoes.

Bring the tomato mixture to a boil. Boil over high heat, stirring very often, until thickencd, about 45 to 50 minutes. Remove the spice bag. Pour into hot jars and seal. Yield: 5 pints.

PICKLES, RELISHES AND CHUTNEYS

From the end of the summer way into the chill of October, kitchens all over the country are filled with the most exciting of all food fragrances — fruit and tomatoes and spices of all kinds simmering in white or golden vinegar sugar syrup: rosy crabapples, golden peaches, chutney relishes, crisp pickled onions, fruit and vegetable relishes, and so many more. How much and how often we depend through the winter on spiced and pickled fruits and vegetables to give a special color and lift to our food.

The history of food reveals that man craved and sought after condiments, salt, vinegar, spices and onions as far back as records extend. These were the substances that added relish and interest to food. It has changed little.

In our Colonial period pickles were highly regarded as they were the only zestful, juicy, crunchy or green colored vegetable available during the winter months.

It was homemade fare for many years, and it was William Underwood who started the commercial processing in 1821, in Boston. It travelled quickly to Canada to New England. The firm is still in business but producing almost only its famous Devilled Ham. Mr. Underwood was followed by Heinz in 1893. At the time it was the ambition of all youngsters to wear a little green pickle pin, which they could obtain at the country summer fair. Then commercial pickling was on its way. After all, pickles are international favorites.

In spite of the easily available variety one can buy, there is still many a woman who seems to enjoy a spice scented kitchen at pickling time. I am one. There are a number of reasons. It is a gratifying hobby; it can also be an economic need to provide for large families at the lowest cost; one may want to use fresh home grown garden produce; and last but not least, many women rise to the challenge of producing interesting, tasty pickles with a personal touch.

A Few Steps to Success

— Follow the recipe exactly. Unless the vinegar, sugar and salt are used in the proper proportion, the pickles will not be of top quality. Too strong a solution produces soft, shrivelled pickles, too weak a solution may spoil them.

— Use only distilled white vinegar, except for special recipes which may call for cider or malt, the last producing a mellow flavor and aroma, but they slightly darken the finished product.

— Do not use table salt, iodized or otherwise, use only coarse salt. The Kosher type is the best, and is easily available through all chain stores across the country.

— Use whole spices when possible as they do not darken the finished product.

— Fill jars, for most pickles, to within ½ inch of the

top, then see that the pickling solution covers the material and is ¼ inch from the top.
— Store in a cool dry place and remember that pickles have a better blended, more mellow flavor when permitted to stand for at least 2 months.

ICE WATER SWEET PICKLES

An old standby, keeps extremely well, and can be done in 20 minutes of work. Add ¼ cup to your beef stew in the winter.

4 cups, unpeeled, sliced cucumbers
1 large onion, sliced
1 tbsp. mustard seed
1 tsp. celery seed
1 cup vinegar
1 tbsp. salt
1 cup sugar
¼ tsp. curry powder

Place sliced cucumbers in a dish, completely cover with ice cubes, then add water to the top. Let stand 2 hours. Drain thoroughly and mix with the sliced onions, mustard seeds and celery seeds. Pack into sterilized jars.

Heat vinegar with the salt, sugar and curry powder. When boiling, pour over cucumbers. Seal. Keep in a cool, dark place. Yield: 2 pints.

QUICK DILL PICKLES

If you grow your own dill, easily done, even on a small patch of earth, or if you buy it at the market, you will enjoy a few jars of homemade dill pickles. They have something quite special.

4 lbs. of 3 to 4-inch cucumbers
6 tbsp. coarse salt
3 cups white vinegar
3 cups water
7 heads of dill or ½ cup dried dill seeds
1 tsp. peppercorns
garlic (optional)

Scrub the cucumbers, rinse 3 to 4 times under running cold water. Cut each cucumber in half, lengthwise.

Combine salt, vinegar and water and bring to a boil. Pack cucumbers into hot sterilized jars. Place a head of dill in each jar or divide the dried dill seeds, then divide the peppercorns and the garlic amongst the jars. Pour in the boiling solution to completely cover the cucumbers. Adjust the lids.

Place jars in a deep saucepan, cover with hot (not boiling) water, the water must come right over the jars. Bring to the boil, cover and boil 10 minutes. Remove jars from water. Set on a tray to cool, then keep in a dark, cool place. Yield: 7 pints.

JIFFY SWEET PICKLES

The overnight treatment is what gives them crispness.
2 quarts small gherkins
½ cup coarse salt
2 quarts water
6 cups brown sugar
1 quart cider vinegar

94

1 tbsp. whole cloves
½ tbsp. celery seeds
½ tbsp. mustard seeds
1 stick cinnamon
bay leaves

Wash the small gherkins and let soak overnight in a brine made with the water and salt, refrigerated.

The next morning drain the gherkins, rinse under hot water and drain again. In a large kettle, bring the brown sugar and vinegar to a boil. Add the gherkins and spices, the latter in a cotton bag. Remove from heat and cool the gherkins in the syrup.

Remove the spice bag, place the pickles in pint jars. Add 1 bay leaf to each jar. According to taste, 1 hot pepper may also be added. Bring the syrup to a boil and fill the jars to the brim. Seal. Yield: 4 pints.

PICKLED DILL CARROTS AND CELERY

Crunchy, tasty little sticks of uncooked carrots and celery can be served with cocktails, seafoods or chicken salad. Most elegant as a picnic vegetable.

4 cups thin long carrot sticks
4 cups thin long celery sticks
2 cups cider vinegar
4 cups water
1 cup sugar
½ cup chilled dill or 2 tbsp. dill seeds
2 tbsp. mustard seeds
1 tbsp. salt
¼ tsp. Tabasco

Cut the sticks of carrot and celery over a bowl of ice water. When all done, drain in a colander and pack together or separately the celery and carrots into 8-ounce jars. (I use empty instant coffee jars, as their height is perfect.)

Combine remaining ingredients in a saucepan, stir until the sugar is dissolved and bring to a rolling boil. Pour hot over the carrots and celery. Cover and keep refrigerated for 2 to 3 days before using. Yield: 8 cups.

DILLED GREEN TOMATOES

Easy and quick to make, they keep well, make use of small green tomatoes and are a pleasant change from dilled cucumbers.

6 quarts small green tomatoes
1 head dill for each quart
12 cups water
4 cups vinegar
1 cup coarse salt

Scrub tomatoes thoroughly and remove stem end. Rinse at least twice and pack closely into quart sealers. Place a good-sized head of dill on top of each.

Bring to a boil the water, vinegar and salt. Pour over the green tomatoes. Seat the jars and store in a cool, dark place for at least 6 weeks before opening. They will keep 6 to 7 months.

If no dark place is available, wrap each jar with newspaper. Yield: 8 quarts.

EASY SWEET MUSTARD PICKLE

One of the best mustard pickles, so quickly done, a must on my yearly pickling list. It costs only a fraction of the commercial type.

6 lbs. of 5 to 6-inch cucumbers
⅔ cup chopped green pepper
6 medium-sized onions
1½ cups diced celery
¼ cup prepared mustard
4⅔ cups white vinegar
½ cup salt
3½ cups sugar
2 tbsp. mustard seed
1 tsp. turmeric
½ tsp. whole cloves

Wash the cucumbers thoroughly. Slice as thinly as possible. Mix in a large bowl the green pepper, onions and celery. In a large saucepan, blend the prepared mustard with the vinegar. Add the salt, sugar and mustard seed, turmeric and whole cloves. Mix well and add the vegetables. Cover and slowly bring to the boil, then simmer, while quickly packing into 1 hot sterilized jar at a time. Fill jars to overflowing and be sure the vinegar solution completely covers the vegetables in each jar. Seal each jar at once. Yield: 9 pints.

SWEET PICKLED SECKEL PEARS

These dainty little pears are on the market around November. Delicious with meat.

97

8 lbs. Seckel pears
water
10 two-inch sticks cinnamon
2 tbsp. whole cloves
2 tbsp. whole allspice
9 cups sugar
1 quart cider vinegar

Wash the pears, remove the blossom ends only and prick the skins with a pointed knife. Place in a saucepan with just enough water to cover. Bring to the boil and boil 10 minutes. Drain.

Tie the spices in a cheesecloth. Combine the sugar and vinegar with 2 cups cold water. Add the spices, bring to a boil, boil 5 minutes. Add the pears, cover and boil 10 minutes, over medium heat, or until pears are tender. Let stand overnight.

In the morning, pack the pears in hot sterile jars. Return syrup to a full rolling boil and pour it over the pears, filling the jars to the top. Seal. Yield: 8 pints.

PICKLED BEETS

A popular old Canadian pickle. Nothing better can be found to serve with corned beef hash or Québec Fricassée. When a jar is empty, I use the vinegar to pickle hard cooked eggs — just boil them and add. Nice to eat with crackers and a salad.

8 cups cooked beets, whole or sliced
2 cups white vinegar
½ cup sugar
1 tsp. salt

16 whole cloves
1 bay leaf

Boil together 10 minutes the vinegar, sugar, salt, cloves and bay leaf.

Beets are left whole when they are small. When large, cut them with a ridged cutter for a fancy appearance or slice plain. They can also be cut into large dice.

Add cooked prepared beets to the hot syrup. Bring to a boil and seal in hot jars. Yield: 2 quarts.

SPICED PICKLED BEETS

Delicious served with tourtière (Quebec meat pie).

3 cups hot cooked beets, sliced
½ cup white vinegar
½ cup water
4 whole cloves
1 stick cinnamon
2 tsp. sugar
1 clove garlic (optional)

Place in a saucepan all the ingredients except the beets. Simmer 8 minutes. Place the beets in hot jars, pour the hot vinegar over. Cover and keep in a cool dark place. Yield: 3 8-oz. jars.

FRESH CANTALOUP PICKLES

My favorite pickle with chicken or ham. Only the fruit is served. I keep the spiced syrup to use as a ham glaze in the winter. Also quite interesting used as a basting sauce on barbecued chicken or spareribs.

1 large unripe cantaloup
white vinegar
brown sugar
8 whole cloves
½ tsp. ground cinnamon
¼ tsp. mace

Peel the cantaloup, remove the seeds, cut into small pieces or into fancy shapes with a small cookie cutter. Place in a bowl and pour vinegar on top until completely covered. Then pour off the vinegar and measure it.

To 2 cups of vinegar, add the remaining ingredients — repeat the same quantity of remaining ingredients for each additional 2 cups of vinegar. Bring the mixture to a fast rolling boil. Add cantaloup and simmer over low heat, uncovered, until almost transparent, about 35 to 40 minutes. Remove cantaloup to a bowl with a slotted spoon. Boil the syrup another 10 minutes. Pour over the cantaloup. Cool and bottle. Let stand 12 hours before using. When packed in sterilized jars, these will keep on a pantry shelf for 5 to 6 months. Yield: 4 cups.

PICKLED CRABAPPLES

An old time taste and delicious. This recipe will be your passport to appreciative thanks whenever you serve it. Refrigerate 24 hours before serving whenever possible.

5 lbs. crabapples
1 quart cider vinegar
3 lbs. sugar
1 tbsp. whole cloves
1 tbsp. cracked cinnamon stick

Wash crabapples in 3 successive baths of cold water. When possible leave the stems on, remove just a small bit of the blossom end. Prick each fruit several times with a sharp-pointed fork. Place in a large saucepan the vinegar, sugar, whole cloves and cracked cinnamon. Slowly bring to a fast rolling boil, stirring often. Boil 10 minutes. At this point you may add a few drops of red coloring, which will give brightness to the crabapples. Add the crabapples to the syrup, then cook over low heat until the fruit is tender. The slow cooking prevents the crabapples from breaking. Pack the crabapples in hot, sterilized jars, fill to overflowing with hot syrup. Seal at once. Yield: 4 pints.

PICKLED CAULIFLOWER

To keep as white as commercial pickled cauliflower, chemical preservatives are needed but the flavor is better without.

2 cauliflowers
coarse salt
4 cups white vinegar
¼ ounce peppercorns
¼ ounce allspice, whole
½ stick cinnamon

Separate the cauliflower into flowerets. Spread out on a large platter and sprinkle with coarse salt. Let stand for 2 days.

Add the spices to the vinegar and boil for 15 minutes. Drain the cauliflower then place in jars and pour the hot vinegar over.

Spread a cloth on top of the jars. Cool before sealing. Yield: 2 pints.

SPECIAL SPICED CRABAPPLES

Because of their fresh flavor and bright color, I prepare and freeze quite a few of these each autumn to use for special dinners during the Christmans period.

16 small ripe crabapples
½ cup sugar
½ cup cold water
6 whole cloves
10 coriander seeds
pinch of salt
3 strips lemon peel

Use firm crabapples. Wash and remove blossom ends, but leave the stems on. Place the remaining ingredients in a saucepan. Stir until the sugar is well mixed. Bring to a boil.

Prick each apple in several places with a knitting pin and place in the saucepan upright, one next to the other. Cover and cook 10 minutes over low heat. Do not stir or uncover. If the heat is low, the apples will be tender but will not burst. Remove from heat and set in a cool place until cold. Do not disturb the apples. When cold, pick up apples by the stems and pack in a freezer container, stagger them so that the second layer fits between stems of the first layer. Strain the juice over the apples. Seal and freeze. To serve, let thaw 1 to 2 hours. Yield: 1 pint.

PICKLED MUSHROOMS

Every year I make two to three dozen jars of pickled mushrooms that I keep in a cool room. I have yet to lose a jar and so I can assure you they will keep for a year. What a pleasure they are to serve as you would pickles!

1 lb. very fresh button mushrooms
1 medium-sized onion, thinly sliced
1 tsp. salt
½ cup water
¾ cup cider or white wine vinegar
10 peppercorns
8 whole cloves allspice
2 bay leaves

Place in a stainless steel or enamel cast iron saucepan (do not use aluminum) the whole mushrooms, onion, salt and water. Cover and simmer over medium low heat 15 to 20 minutes. Add the vinegar, peppercorns, allspice and bay leaves. Simmer 3 minutes longer. Cool. Divide mushrooms equally into small glass jars. Cover with the hot liquid. Seal tightly. Keep in a cool dark place or refrigerate. Yield: 4 cups.

PICKLED SILVER SKIN ONIONS

I have been asked more often for pickled onions than any other type. The ice water treatment is the secret of crisp white onions.

4 quarts small pickling onions
boiling water

cold water
ice cubes
1 cup coarse salt
¼ cup pickling spices (optional)
2 quarts white vinegar
2 cups sugar

Pour enough boiling water over the unpeeled onions so that they will be well covered. Let stand exactly 5 minutes. Drain. Pour cold water on top and peel. Place in a large bowl. Sprinkle with the coarse salt and completely cover with ice cubes. Let stand overnight in as cool a place as possible.

Next day, drain the onions, rinse thoroughly in ice water, drain again.

Tie the pickling spices in a cotton bag. Boil with the vinegar and sugar for 5 minutes after the mixture starts to boil. Remove spice bag. Add onions to boiling liquid, boil exactly 2 minutes. Pour into clean hot jars, fill to overflowing with the hot vinegar. Seal at once. Store at least 1 month before using. Yield: 6 to 7 pints.

GINGER PEAR SWEET PICKLES

Served with your Christmas turkey or Easter ham, they will be a conversation piece. In the fall I use Bartlett pears, in the winter I like Comice or Bosc pears.

2½ lbs. fresh pears, ripe but firm
1 tsp. whole cloves
½ cup shredded ginger, fresh, preserved or candied
3 cups sugar

2 unpeeled lemon, thinly sliced and seeded
red vegetable coloring to taste

Wash, pare, quarter and core the pears. Slice ¼ inch thick directly into a non-metal bowl. Add the cloves, ginger and sugar. Stir until thoroughly mixed. Cover and let stand overnight. In the morning pour the mixture into a saucepan, bring *slowly* to the boil. Add the lemon slices, cut in half, and boil slowly 5 minutes. Add a few drops of red coloring if you wish, but do it cautiously so that the pickle will have only a faint blush of color. Cook over low heat, stirring occasionally, until the pears are translucent and tender and the syrup is somewhat thickened, this will take about 1½ hours. What makes this pickle perfect is the long slow cooking. Remove from heat. Cool, then cover and let stand until the next day, when each piece of fruit will be plump and the syrup quite thick. Fill hot sterilized jars, seal. Yield: 3 half pints.

CANNED PLUM PICKLES

No time? Then use canned purple plums. In 5 minutes, you can make a good relish, delicious with any roast, perfect with ham and pork.

2 cans (16 ounces each) purple plums
2 sweet pickles
French dressing of your choice
½ tsp. curry powder
grated rind of an orange

Drain plums, remove pits, cut in small pieces, chop pickles, mix with plums. Add 2 to 3 tablespoons of a

105

French dressing of your choice, the curry and orange rind. Beat together until well mixed. Let stand 12 to 24 hours before serving. Stir well when ready to serve. Yield: about 1½ cups.

PICKLED PLUMS

This pickle is delicious with cheese or in fruit salad. Equally good made with the purple plums or the Damson plums.

4 lbs. plums
1½ lbs. sugar
1½ cups cider vinegar
1 4-inch stick cinnamon
18 whole cloves

Wash and prick each plum 3 to 4 times with a sharp knitting pin. Stick a clove into 18 of the plums and place them all in a bowl.

Bring to a boil the sugar, vinegar and cinnamon stick. Boil for 15 minutes and pour boiling hot over the plums. Cover with a wax paper and let stand overnight. The next day pour all of it into a saucepan and bring to a full rolling boil.

Remove plums with a perforated ladle and pack equally into hot sterilized jars. Fill each to overflowing with the boiling syrup. Seal. Keep in cool, dark place. Yield: 3 to 4 5-ounce jars.

PICKLED GREEN GINGER PLUMS

Another colorful and different pickle to serve with roasted chicken or duck and as a garnish to winter fruit salad.

8 to 9 cups large, firm green gage plums
½ cup candied diced ginger
3½ cups sugar
2 cups white vinegar
1 stick cinnamon
1 tsp. whole cloves
1 tsp. allspice
½ tsp. cardamom seeds (out of the shell)
¼ tsp. coriander seeds

Wash the plums and leave whole. Make a syrup with the sugar and vinegar. Place the spices in a cheesecloth bag. Add to the boiling syrup, boil 5 minutes. Add the plums, one by one, and the ginger to the syrup. Bring back to a slow boil. Simmer gently until the plums are tender without being all broken up. Avoid overcooking. Seal in hot sterilized jars, well covered with syrup. Yield: 6 pints.

PICKLED PUMPKIN

This recipe hails from a young mother, who has used it to pickle her Halloween pumpkin, very good with roasted birds of all types.

1 pint white or cider vinegar
4 lbs. sugar
1 tsp. whole cloves
1 tbsp. broken cinnamon stick
5 lbs. pumpkin, pared and cut in 1-inch cubes

Place in a large saucepan the vinegar and sugar. Tie the whole cloves and cinnamon stick in cotton. Add to the vinegar. Slowly bring to the boil, while stirring, then boil 5 minutes. Add the pumpkin and cook 10 to 15 minutes or until tender. Place pumpkin in hot jars, cover each with syrup and seal. Yield: 5 pints.

QUINCE PICKLE

These beautiful apricot or peach colored and flavored fruits are never in quantity on the market, but when you find them, pickle them to keep as your favorite fruit salad garnish and a very special pickle.

8 quince
whole cloves
2 oranges, unpeeled
6 cups sugar
2 cups cider or white vinegar
1 3-inch stick of cinnamon
1 firm apple

Peel, core and quarter quince. Stick 2 cloves into each piece. Place in a saucepan, just cover with a little water and cook until tender, drain, reserving the liquid.

Slice the oranges as thinly as possible, remove the seeds, peel, core and dice apple.

Place in a saucepan the sliced oranges, sugar, vinegar, 1½ cups reserved liquid from the quince, cinnamon and apple. Simmer 15 minutes over low heat. Add quince and keep simmering gently for 25 to 30 minutes, a nice compote will form around the quince. Fill hot sterilized jars with fruits and cover with syrup to within ⅛ of an inch from top. Make sure syrup covers fruit completely. Seal. Yield: 6 pints.

PICKLED TURNIPS

A friend, expert in Arabic cooking, showed me how to pickle small white or medium yellow turnips. They are most attractive to look at, have a delicious flavor, and are particularly good with highly seasoned foods, all barbecued foods, and with rice or barley dishes — they never fail to be a conversation piece.

6 to 8 small to medium turnips
1 beet, uncooked, peeled
2 cups water
1 cup cider or red wine vinegar
2 to 3 cloves garlic, left whole
2 tsp. salt
2 small pods of dried hot peppers

Peel the turnips, then cut in the following manner. Remove a slice from the top and bottom to make the turnip even. Then slice lengthwise into 1/4-inch sticks to within 1/2 inch of the bottom. The point is not to separate the slices from each other — all the sticks remain attached to the base. Place in bowls, completely cover with cold water and let stand overnight. Rinse in 5 to 6 waters in the morning.

Slice the uncooked beet and place half in the bottom of a large-mouthed glass jar. Top with the rinsed turnips and place the remaining beet on top.

Stir the remaining ingredients together and pour over the beet. Cover. Store in a cool place. Let stand at least

3 days, 6 if possible, shaking the bottle 5 to 6 times, so that the beet coloring gets evenly distributed through the turnip. Yield: about 3 pints.

GRAPE KETCHUP

Grape ketchup is as good and as elegant as the English walnut ketchup. Serve with game, wild birds and pork, or spread on bread to eat with cheese.

5 lbs. Blue Concord grapes
2 lbs. light brown sugar
1 tbsp. ground cloves
1 tbsp. cinnamon
1 tbsp. pepper
1 tbsp. allspice
1 tsp. salt
1 pint red wine or malt vinegar

Pluck grapes from stems. Place in a saucepan, cover and simmer, stirring a few times, for 10 minutes or until juicy and boiling. Pass through a fine sieve, to remove the seeds.

Place the purée in the saucepan, add the brown sugar, cloves, cinnamon, pepper, allspice, salt and vinegar. Boil gently until thickened, from 40 to 60 minutes, stir often to prevent sticking. Pour into sterilized ketchup bottles and seal. Let stand 4 to 5 weeks before using. Yield: 6 pints.

WHITE AND GREEN RELISH

Each year I like to double and triple this recipe as I never seem to have enough. I use it in many ways. In the winter, I love a spoonful added to French dressing or mixed with cream cheese to spread over hot oatmeal bread, where its green and white and red color comes out beautifully.

4 cups diced celery (no leaves)
1 cup chopped white onions
2 large green peppers, seeded and diced
2 large red sweet peppers, seeded and diced
2 cups white vinegar
½ cup sugar
1 tsp. salt
1 tsp. dry mustard

Cook celery and onions 10 minutes in a small amount of water salted with coarse salt. Drain, place in a large saucepan. Add all the other ingredients. Boil until all the vegetables are tender and texture is good. Seal in hot sterilized jars. Yield: 3 pints.

INDIA RELISH

This fashionable relish of the 1900's has lost none of its glamor, but is too often forgotten. Serve it with a lot of dishes but remember it is perfect with fish and salad dressing.

8 lbs. very small green tomatoes
8 cups light brown sugar
2 cups water
3 sticks cinnamon
2 tbsp. ground ginger
3 lemons, unpeeled, thinly sliced

2 cups candied citron, diced
3 cups seedless raisins
grated peel of 1 orange

Wash the tomatoes, remove the stems and cut into quarters.

Make a syrup with sugar and water, add the tomatoes, cinnamon, ginger, lemon slices, citron, raisins and grated orange peel. Bring to a boil and boil slowly until the tomatoes are transparent and the lemon slices are clear. Pour into hot sterilized containers and seal. Yield: 6 quarts.

GREEN GINGER PEAR RELISH

Here green ginger is a must. Easy to find in Oriental food shops. A perfect relish with meat, equally at home with toast or hot biscuits at tea time.

4 lbs. fresh pears (any type)
½ cup peeled and grated green ginger root
¼ cup fresh lemon juice
5 cups sugar
grated rind of 1 lemon
¼ cup cider vinegar

Wash, peel, quarter and core pears. Place in cold salted water as ready, to prevent discoloration. Place the grated ginger in the lemon juice. Place the drained pears in a glass bowl, sprinkle the sugar on top gradually, mixing well to coat each piece. Cover and let stand 6 to 8 hours.

When ready, stir in the pears, and the lemon ginger mixture. Cook uncovered over medium low heat until the pears are tender and clear. This should take about 1 hour, stirring frequently. Add grated lemon peel and vinegar about 5 minutes before cooking period is over.

Pack in hot, sterilized jars, filling them to within ½ inch of top. Seal at once. Yield: 6 half pints.

APPLE CHUTNEY

An interesting winter spicy relish, that even improves as it ages. Serve with turkey, lamb, kidney of all types and, of course, any curried dish.

> **2 lbs. cooking apples**
> **3 medium-sized onions**
> **½ cup brown sugar**
> **1 tsp. salt**
> **½ tsp. pickling spices**
> **½ tsp. ground ginger**
> **½ tsp. ground coriander**
> **1 cup cider vinegar**
> **⅔ cup molasses**

Peel and core the apples, chopped fine. Peel and chop the onions. Place both in a saucepan (enamel cast iron is the best type). Add the brown sugar, salt, pickling spices, ginger, coriander, vinegar and molasses. Stir until thoroughly mixed.

Bring to a boil over medium heat, stirring often. Then, simmer uncovered over low heat for 2 hours, stirring often, or until it comes to a jam consistency. Cool, pour into sterilized jars. Cover. Yield: 3 pints.

PLUM CHUTNEY

Make this winter chutney to serve with the Christmas turkey or a roasted leg of lamb. Give it five to six weeks to ripen.

3 lbs. prune plums
1 lb. green apples
1 large onion
1 oz. preserved ginger
2 cups sugar
2 tsp. salt
¼ tsp. cayenne
1 tbsp. mixed pickling spices
2 cups vinegar

Cut stoned plums into small pieces, peel and chop apples and onions. Chop ginger fine, tie spices in a cheesecloth bag. Combine all ingredients in a large saucepan.

Place over low heat, cook slowly until chutney is of good consistency, about 2 to 2½ hours. Turn into hot sterilized jars, seal firmly tight. Yield: 6 5-oz. jars.

PLUM AND TOMATO CHUTNEY

I have made and kept this chutney as long as 3 years — it improves with age. Good with so many types of dishes: curry, roasted chicken, roast pork, cold cuts, lamb, stew, etc.

2 lbs. freestone blue plums
1 lb. red or green tomatoes
4 onions, chopped
1tbsp. salt

½ cup seedless raisins
2 tbsp. curry powder
⅛ tsp. cayenne pepper
2 tbsp. ground ginger or ¼ cup fresh ginger, grated
1½ cups cider or white vinegar
2 cups brown sugar

Cut up the plums and discard the pits. Scald and skin the red tomatoes (not the green). Chop coarsely.

Place the plums and tomatoes in a saucepan with the remaining ingredients. Bring to a full rolling boil, while stirring constantly, then boil gently over medium heat for 1 hour or until it has a good consistency. Cool. Pour into sterilized jars. Seal. Yield: about 4 pints.

UNCOOKED RELISHES

NO COOKING CHOW-CHOW

Economical and easy to make, a perfect relish with meat loaf, hamburgers and frankfurters.

> 2 large heads of cabbage, cut in pieces
> 6 large onions, peeled
> 6 green peppers, cleaned of seeds
> 6 large apples, cored, unpeeled
> ¾ cup coarse salt
> 3 quarts white vinegar
> 3 lbs. light brown sugar
> 2 tbsp. celery seed
> 2 tbsp. mustard seed

Pass through a coarse grinder or vegetable shredder the cabbage, onions, green peppers and apples. Place in a large bowl (do not use metal) or crock. Add the coarse salt. Mix thoroughly. Cover with a cloth and let stand overnight.

In another bowl mix together the vinegar, brown sugar, celery seeds and mustard seeds and also let stand overnight.

In the morning, drain the vegetables, add them to the vinegar mixture. Let stand 12 hours. Then stir thoroughly and pack into sterilized jars and seal. Yield: 5 quarts.

BARBECUE RELISH

Mostly from the pantry shelf, a quickly made relish which can be a hostess' best friend for an unexpected barbecue party or to serve with baked spareribs.

1 cup ketchup or chili sauce
½ cup minced mild onions or green onions
1 small green pepper, grated
¼ cup finely chopped olives
½ tsp. marjoram or dill

Combine and thoroughly mix all the ingredients. Place in a covered dish or jar. When time permits, refrigerate 1 hour before serving. Yield: about 2 cups.

CHUTNEY ON THE GO

In India, chutney is a must. Bottled types are mostly prepared from seasonal fruits but a fresh chutney is usually used and their collection is endless. Excellent with barbecued meats and roast pork as well as curried dishes. The cardamon and cumin can be replaced by 1 teaspoon of curry powder.

2 large tomatoes
1 tbsp. brown sugar
1 large green sweet pepper
1 large red sweet pepper*
1 onion, chopped fine

*All green or all red peppers can be used.

1 cup fresh lemon juice
grated rind of 1 lemon
½ tsp. ground cardamom
½ tsp. cumin seeds
½ cup minced parsley

Dice the unpeeled tomatoes, sprinkle with the brown sugar. Dice the green and red sweet pepper and the onion, add to the tomatoes. Stir gently to blend.

To the lemon juice, add the lemon rind, cardamom, cumin and parsley. Stir together for a few seconds. Blend into the vegetable mixture. Cover and stir occasionally at room temperature for 1 hour. Refrigerate until well chilled as it should be served cold with hot food. Yield: 3½ to 4 cups.

SUMMER CHUTNEY

This superb chutney needs only to be stirred together and served, and it can be made from ingredients that can be constantly part of the emergency shelf.

1 cup chutney (any type)
1 cup red or black currant jelly
⅓ cup sherry
1 tbsp. Worcestershire or H.P. Sauce

Stir together all the ingredients until thoroughly blended. Chill and serve. Yield: 2 cups.

SALT PICKLED EGGS, GIPSY STYLE

These are golden color with a special flavor taken from the onion skins and caraway seeds. They make an interesting hors d'oeuvre before an informal garden dinner, or to serve with a green salad, or just to munch with soda crackers and a cool glass of beer.

12 hard cooked eggs
¼ cup coarse salt
1 cup dry yellow onion skins
2 tsp. caraway seeds
4 cups water

Cool the hot hard cooked eggs under running cold water and tap the shells all over to crack, but do not peel.

Place in a glass jar or pyrex bowl.

Place the salt, onion skins, caraway seeds and water in a saucepan. Bring to a fast rolling boil and boil 5 minutes. Pour boiling hot over the eggs. Cover. Let cool. Then chill for 24 hours. Peel and serve whole, halved, or quartered. If any remain, keep in a glass jar without liquid, well covered, and refrigerate. Yield: 12 eggs.

INDEX